The Executive's Guide to Account-Based Marketing: Grow your most valuable customers

The Executive's Guide to Account-Based Marketing: Grow your most valuable customers

Brought to you by Momentum ITSMA, the global pioneers of Account-Based Marketing (ABM), this guide will help you build an account-based strategy, create powerful customer collaboration, and drive sustained revenue growth.

Alisha Lyndon

Contents

Contributors   ix

Foreword   xiii

1. What is Account-Based Marketing?   **1**

Key principles   2

Attributes of an Account-Based Marketing strategy   5

Account-Based Marketing in action   7

Anatomy of an Account-Based Marketing success   9

2. The case for change   **11**

Shifting trends in the customer-supplier dynamic   12

Account-Based Marketing works   17

Technology makes Account-Based Marketing easier   19

The benefits for your customers, teams and company   21

3.   The impact of Account-Based Marketing strategies   **23**

How to measure results   25

Measurement framework   26

What results can you expect?   28

4.   Lessons learned from designing and implementing programs   **31**

Myth 1: Account-Based Marketing is a personalization tool   32

Myth 2: Account-Based Marketing is a one-size-fits-all solution   34

Myth 3: Account-Based Marketing is just another name for Key Account Management   35

5.   Designing your Account-Based Marketing strategy   **37**

Strategic account selection   39

Highly-customized growth plans for individual accounts   40

Marketing, sales and delivery team collaboration   42

Account-Based Marketing for multiple accounts   43

6.   Critical success factors   **45**

Dimension 1: Strategic Alignment   46

Dimension 2: Objectives and Metrics   48

Dimension 3: Account selection and segmentation   50

Dimension 4: Content and campaigns   52

Dimension 5: Program operations and resources   54

Dimension 6: Data, Analytics, and Insight   56

Dimension 7: Technology Infrastructure   58

7. How to embed an Account-Based Marketing strategy   61

Stage 1. Exploring   65

Stage 2. Experimenting   66

Stage 3. Expanding   67

Stage 4. Embedded   68

8. How to accelerate your Account-Based Marketing   69

Maturity matters   71

A roadmap for success   73

About the author   76

About Momentum ITSMA   77

Contributors

Rob Leavitt, Senior Vice President, Momentum ITSMA

Rob works with a wide range of Momentum ITSMA's customers to advance marketing maturity and support transformations that drive business impact. He oversees several research studies and publications and is a subject matter expert on Growth Hub. Rob is also a regular industry speaker and hosts Momentum ITSMA's C-Suite Marketing Podcast.

Before rejoining Momentum ITSMA in 2016, Rob led thought leadership and marketing programs for PTC Global Services. Prior to PTC, he consulted with a variety of technology and professional services firms on marketing strategy, thought leadership, customer collaboration, and other issues. Before succumbing to the lure of high tech in the late 1990s, Rob ran a variety of international media and education programs, and he continues to serve on several nonprofit boards today. He has a BA in American History from the University of Pennsylvania and a Master's degree in Political Science from MIT.

Robert Hollier, Partner, Momentum ITSMA

Since 2012, Robert has been advising Momentum ITSMA's customers on how to transform their go-to-market strategies, shape better-crafted customer conversations, and enable sales teams to increase win rates. Robert also leads The Momentum ITSMA Customer Buying Index (CBX), now in its 20th year, a global research study of CxO buyers in the top 2,000 firms to better understand which sales and marketing strategies are leading to revenue growth.

Robert brings more than 25 years of experience in marketing, having held several marketing leadership positions at organizations including Cisco, and he also launched a London-based public relations and content firm. He holds a BA with honours in English Language and Literature from University College, Oxford, and has an MSc in Information Systems.

Dave Munn, Chief Community Officer, Momentum ITSMA

Dave has spent more than 25 years leading the way in defining, documenting, and inspiring marketing excellence and transformation across the B2B marketing profession. Today, he leads Momentum ITSMA's global community, Growth Hub.

Dave advises marketing leaders across Growth Hub on a range of topics, chairing Momentum ITSMA's advisory boards and councils, and leading the firm's flagship events, Marketing Vision and Marketing Leadership Forum. Dave helped pioneer the discipline of Account-Based Marketing (ABM) in the early 2000s and is co-author of *A Practitioner's Guide to ABM: Accelerating Growth in Strategic Accounts* (Kogan Page, 2017) and the new, updated Second Edition of *A Practitioner's Guide to ABM* (Kogan Page, 2021).

Before joining ITSMA in 1995, Dave held senior-level field positions with Oracle and Apple, where he was responsible for marketing to commercial and government accounts. Earlier, Dave was a senior analyst with The Ledgeway Group, which is now part of Gartner, where he authored Ledgeway's first Service Trends and Forecast study. He holds a Bachelor of Arts degree in Economics from Denison University and an MBA from Northwestern University's Kellogg School, where he concentrated on Marketing and Corporate Strategy. He lives in historic Concord, Massachusetts.

This book draws on two studies from Momentum ITSMA:

CBX, Momentum ITSMA's study into buying cycles

This study provides a rolling pulse of how executives engage suppliers, changes in buying processes and identifies the most effective actives leading to revenue. It is conducted every six months with c-suite decision makers from enterprises across the global 2,000, on investment decisions of $500K.

ABX, Momentum ITSMA's annual ABM benchmarking study

This annual study is conducted in partnership with the ABM leadership alliance and is now in it's 6th year. The study is conducted with over 300 marketing leaders across B2B and is supported by qualitative interviews.

Foreword

My passion for Account-Based Marketing started after I heard about a sales rep from a top technology firm going in to see a CIO at a global bank, and ending the meeting by placing a stack of brochures on the customer desk as if to imply "you might find something interesting in here."

Far too many sales and marketing teams have been focused on what they have to sell, not putting enough emphasis on understanding what's going on with their customer's business and figuring out where they can add the most value.

> *Account-Based Marketing is a strategy that helps organizations to treat customers as markets of one, making the most of customer insights to build tailored value propositions and develop specific engagement strategies.*

TAKEAWAY

Over the past few decades, many of the world's largest and leading companies have adopted Account-Based Marketing strategies, building dedicated teams and embedding a customer-focused approach across the go-to-market.

Our consulting work and the *Momentum ITSMA account-based benchmarking study* (2021) have shown that ABM delivers big business outcomes, 73% of firms see measurable impact in account relationships, 65% see revenue growth and 40% see quantifiable improvement in their reputation across their most strategic accounts.

Today, with competition intensifying and complexity increasing, organizations are finding it harder to expand their share of wallet in high-value accounts. Our annual buyer research study, *The Momentum ITSMA Customer Buying Index (CBX)*, has highlighted the need for a clear guide to unlocking Account-Based Marketing, with the most recent research indicating buying cycles are becoming increasingly problematic with growing scrutiny of business cases.

This work aims to serve as a guide for executives who want to embed account-based principles within their organization and embrace the strategic importance of expanding business with their most valuable customers.

It shows how account-based strategy can:

- Drive strategic growth in good times and in bad
- Make companies more customer-centric

- Enable collaboration and alignment across the entire organization
- Influence all of marketing by building brand awareness and driving business

With huge thank you to our contributors, Rob Leavitt, Robert Hollier, and Dave Munn. Also, to Jeanne Brown and Alex Koenig, without whom this book would not have been possible.

My hope is that you use this book to help you sharpen your account-based strategy into a full-fledged, organization-wide initiative that drives accelerated growth.

For more resources on this topic, please visit

www.momentumitsma.com

or listen to our management podcast Account-Based Marketing.

Alisha Lyndon, CEO, Momentum ITSMA

1 What is Account-Based Marketing?

Over the past two decades, Account-Based Marketing has taken off as a strategic business imperative. We've seen it capture the hearts and minds of executives due to the long-term business impact it delivers and the alignment it creates between teams of sales and marketing professionals who have been given a framework to more effectively deliver on overall business priorities.

Account-Based Marketing is a strategic approach that treats individual accounts as markets in their own right. It is designed to create sustainable and profitable growth within your most valuable accounts, bringing together the mindset, skills, and resources of your marketing, sales and delivery teams, as well as relevant business leaders, to focus on helping your customer achieve their business goals.

Key principles

There are four underlying principles of Account-Based Marketing:

- **Customer centricity is paramount.** With Account-Based Marketing, sales, marketing, and delivery teams focus on solving the customer's problem, or helping the customer capitlize on market opportunity, rather than promoting the solution they want to sell. This outside-in approach requires developing a deep understanding of each customer and their organization, as well as their pain points and their opportunities, in enough depth to develop solutions that help the account achieve their business objectives.

- **Insight is needed to build relevance.** Using a combination of market insight, account insight, and individual buyer insight, marketing and sales work together to craft value propositions to drive interest and engagement and to make the customer feel as though they are a market of one.

- **Collaboration across sales, marketing, and delivery teams is essential.** Account-Based Marketing will only achieve its potential when teams work hand-in-hand, cross-functionally. This requires more than agreeing upon definitions, rules of engagement, and a list of prioritized accounts. It means that sales, marketing and delivery teams are partners collaborating as one team, and that team has the customer's needs as the top agenda item. In many cases, this mindset will extend to your partner ecosystem.

- **Building reputation and relationships is just as important as generating revenue.** Account-Based Marketing objectives focus on customer lifetime value, going beyond lead generation and this quarter's revenue goal, to drive increased mindshare and stronger, long-term relationships. This may mean putting the customer's goals above your own.

Account-Based Marketing is about people, not personas; accounts, not markets. It shifts the focus from the broadcast of "Let me tell you why we are great," to the value of "We see your problems and opportunities — let us help you get there."

This means shifting your mindset:

From	To
Broad-based campaigns that cast a wide net to 100s accounts, using generic content that leads with an offer	Narrowing the focus to engage directly with priority-named accounts and buying teams, offering relevant content that addresses a specific problem or opportunity
Lead generation with baton passing between marketing and sales	Working as one team to develop opportunities based on the account's biggest needs and highlighting where you can add the most value
Sales and marketing efforts focused on products or solutions	Value-based propositions relevant to each of your accounts
Selling and marketing to stakeholders you already know	Understanding the full buyer landscape to communicate and engage with various buyers at key points of the buyer journey

From	To
Having a sole goal of selling more	Setting an intention to grow within accounts, placing value on building reputation and relationships as well as driving revenue

At its core, Account-Based Marketing is about inspiring your customers with a vision of what is possible and filling them with the confidence that you are the right partner to help them achieve that vision.

Account-Based Marketing starts from a deep-seated understanding of the requirements of individual decision-makers within a business:

- What are they trying to achieve?
- What are their challenges and opportunities?
- What is their vision?
- What is their chosen strategy?
- Who do they collaborate with?

For an organization to realize the full potential of its Account-Based Marketing efforts, everything — from research to value propositions to messaging to designing and implementing campaigns to executing executive conversations — must be shaped around individual accounts, as well as the individual(s) or team(s) who makes or influences the purchasing decision.

Attributes of an Account-Based Marketing strategy:

While Account-Based Marketing shares some characteristics with other growth strategies, it requires a new form of thinking as an end-to-end approach.

An Account-Based Marketing strategy is:

- **Account-centric.** It's not merely about understanding the marketplace or industry; it's about cultivating a deep understanding of the account, individuals and teams, and its place within that market — its strengths, weaknesses, opportunities, and threats — and then helping the account address each of those.

- **People-centric.** It's about truly getting to know each person in the account. If they have influence over the purchasing process, they are the target audience.

- **Long-term.** Account-Based Marketing is about building trust and developing relationships, which takes time. Don't expect short-term returns — if you're in it for the long-term, you'll achieve sustainable results.

- **Cross-functional.** Account-Based Marketing is not the preserve of the marketing department alone. Rather, it should unite sales, marketing and delivery teams.

- **Always on.** Account-Based Marketing is not a one-and-done campaign. It's about nurturing relationships, listening to your customers, and anticipating their needs.

Why adopt Account-Based Marketing as a business strategy?

"ABM at it's core is about understanding your markets and align teams to be customer centric – it also reduces organization silos and helps to focus on what really matters. When ABM is embraced as a business initiative it's drives a stronger impact and should be on every executives radar."

– Claire Darling, Chief Marketing Officer, Skybox

Account-Based Marketing in action

Oracle has successfully implemented an Account-Based Marketing strategy that in one account alone resulted in an increase in revenue from $2m to $29m and has developed 100+ relationships along the way.

Oracle had already been working with a European telecoms giant in one line of business worth about $2M in annualized income, but Oracle saw an opportunity to develop the customer into a key account. Oracle partnered with Momentum ITSMA to implement a strategic Account-Based Marketing approach.

It began by conducting detailed account research to better understand the customer. We held a workshop with Oracle's account team to leverage these insights and identify where they should focus. Working with Oracle's feedback, we created a single narrative that could be used across every interaction with the customer's teams.

Oracle took an "art of the possible" approach with the customer, showing where the account could go and what it could accomplish through a partnership with Oracle. A few stakeholders at the customer showed interest and wanted to see more.

Oracle went on to kick off a series of different activities at the C-suite level and across the customer more broadly. It delivered thought leadership, videos, mobile apps, and workshops, and repackaged existing case studies to be more relevant to the customer. The final piece was a presentation used at board level for sign-off.

This process was not all smooth sailing; about 2/3 of the way through the sales cycle, one of the main decision-makers at the customer left the business. Frequently, a change of this magnitude can stall or derail the deal; however, the new person in the role saw the promise of the solution and ran with it.

Oracle ended up closing a $29M in revenue, engaging with 100 people in the customer, and expanding its presence from a small, siloed area to working on a transformation project.

This example offers key takeaways for any Account-Based Marketing program:

- Engage early with the customer for maximum impact
- Don't just solve problems; identify opportunities for growth
- Lead with evidence-based insight
- Focus on a proactive sales-marketing-delivery team partnership to connect consistently with the customer throughout the buying cycle
- Develop relationships with multiple key stakeholders who can champion your solution

Anatomy of an Account-Based Marketing success

Oracle successfully applied Account-Based Marketing to a telecoms account, resulting in:

- Creating and closing a multi-million-dollar deal despite a change in key stakeholders
- Developing large-scale opportunities in the pipeline
- Gaining buy-in from across the account through to the executive board

Oracle chose to adopt an Account-Based Marketing strategy on this key account for three reasons:

1. To achieve closer alignment between sales and marketing teams
2. To position Oracle's value against the customer's strategic objectives
3. To develop transformational sales opportunities

2 The case for change

Building on its success over the past few decades, as well as changes in the broader marketing and technology environment, Account-Based Marketing is being hailed as the great revolution in driving enterprise revenue growth.

Vendors and pundits alike are making great claims about Account-Based Marketing transforming all of sales and marketing. Adoption of Account-Based Marketing has continued to increase and shows no sign of slowing, with more than half of companies having an established Account-Based Marketing program today, while 15% are piloting programs and another 19% are in the planning stage (Source: *Momentum ITSMA ABX, 2021*). https://momentumitsma.com/embedding-abm-next-steps-for-market-leadership/

There are three clear reasons to invest in Account-Based Marketing:

1. Shifting trends in the customer-supplier dynamic

It's important to understand that your accounts do not stand still. In a world where the only constant is change, it's vital to stay close to the market and be ready to respond to changing buying dynamics.

The clearest example here is the global pandemic that began in 2020. This severely challenged the viability of many businesses and instigated rapid change, including the adoption of hybrid working. Many sales teams and executives found themselves somewhat cut off from their customers, forced to rely on virtual and digital channels. As a result, they needed much more support from marketing to understand customer behaviour and engage customers in relevant new ways.

Momentum ITSMA's Customer Buying Index (CBX) regularly takes the pulse of the Global 2,000 to understand what is changing in their world. We use this study to give our clients' sales and marketing teams insightful analysis and transformative advice.

Our research shows there is a new customer and supplier contract emerging, one that shows customers are more open to sharing information with suppliers, have a growing appetite to hear about innovation from suppliers and are ready to collaborate.

What's changing for the global 2,000?

- Enterprise customers are actively seeking to form deeper and more collaborative partnerships, but with a limited set of solution providers.
- Those same customers are facing new external challenges. Consumer behavior is changing and the macro-economic environment is volatile. This is creating doubt as to whether existing providers have all the capabilities these enterprise accounts need.
- Against that backdrop, incumbent providers need to double down on their existing accounts and dial up their innovation and collaboration messaging.
- Many enterprises face increased scrutiny of the business case for new investment internally and want the help of providers to develop the business case.
- In the uncertain world we currently live in, your executive team is often an untapped source of value for your customers, giving them confidence in your resource, commitment and capabilities. Account-Based Marketing strategies must remain flexible and agile to stay aligned with the evolving needs and requirements of strategic accounts.

Many organizations recognize the need to collaborate more with key customers to accelerate growth and innovation. An Account-Based Marketing strategy is an effective way of getting your go-to-market teams pointing in the same direction and getting them to focus on the same metrics.

Changes in B2B relationships and the complexity of enterprise sales mean that buyer behavior is changing. (Source: *Momentum ITSMA's 2022 CBX Research*)

Consider, for example:

- Your accounts are drowning in content.
- Offerings are commoditized, particularly in industries such as technology where it's harder to tell solutions apart.
- Customers are demanding a more relevant and personalized experience.
- Customers often make it over two-thirds of the way through their buying decisions before they talk to a sales team. More than half of enterprise accounts do not talk to your sales team as one of their first steps when they initiate a buying process.
- In recent years, the number of enterprise accounts conducting their own research on solution providers has accelerated as they increase their efforts to seek advice from industry analysts and the opinion of their peers.
- Decision-making buying teams are growing and becoming more complex, with 42% finding it harder to buy and the pandemic exacerbated this challenge.
- New roles such as the chief digital officer and the chief innovation officer are emerging and proving increasingly influential.

A number of new barriers have emerged to growing revenue in enterprise accounts in a post-covid era:

- **Reduced cut-through.** As tailored information becomes the new normal, customers increasingly expect greater personalization, relevance, and focus on outcomes. In fact, **76%** of buyers say they now receive tailored information from vendors. (Figure 1)

- **Intensifying competition.** A heightened cultural appetite for change and intensifying competition means customers are more willing to switch providers. A full **48%** of enterprises today are more likely to move away from their incumbent provider and choose a new provider.

- **Growing complexity.** Increased scrutiny of the business case and growing complexity in collaboration are blocking

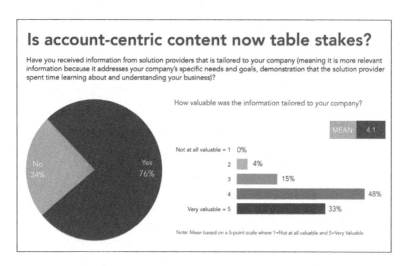

Is account-centric content now table stakes?

Have you received information from solution providers that is tailored to your company (meaning it is more relevant information because it addresses your company's specific needs and goals, demonstration that the solution provider spent time learning about and understanding your business)?

No 34%
Yes 76%

How valuable was the information tailored to your company?

MEAN 4.1

Not at all valuable = 1	0%
2	4%
3	15%
4	48%
Very valuable = 5	33%

Note: Mean based on a 5-point scale where 1=Not at all valuable and 5=Very Valuable

FIGURE 1

Source: *Momentum ITSMA CBX, 2022*

customer's purchase decisions. Nearly half (**45%**) of enterprises say it's more difficult today to make large purchasing decisions than it was in the past.

What activities inspire trust in customers?

Trust is a crucial ingredient to developing strategic customers and deepening relationships. Our most recent wave of CBX shows five successful activities in building trust:

What activities inspire trust in customers?

Trust is a crucial ingredient to developing strategic customers and deepening relationships. Our most recent wave of CBX shows five successful activities in building trust:

45%
Executive-to-executive meetings

37%
High-quality thought leadership

36%
Understanding of my role and personal objectives

30%
Access to product or solution development roadmaps

27%
Special account relationship development programs such as exclusive events

FIGURE 2

Source: *Momentum ITSMA CBX, 2022*

What impact has ABM had?

"As a start-up we have a challenging growth target in Kyndryl; to achieve it we are doubling down on an account-based strategy and making customer centricity the heart of our culture."

— Clara Belalcazar, Chief Marketing Officer US, Kyndryl

2. Account-Based Marketing works

Firms that have implemented Account-Based Marketing with their customers are seeing results and are looking to expand and scale their Account-Based Marketing activities. An impressive 72% of firms reported their Account-Based Marketing strategies outperformed any other marketing investment in terms of ROI. (Figure 3)

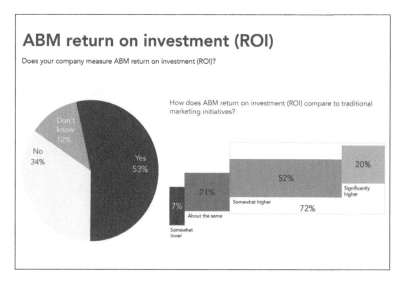

FIGURE 3

Source: *Momentum ITSMA ABM Benchmarking Study*

In the same survey, 65% of respondents indicated Account-Based Marketing is the reason for significant impact in revenue, 40% see an improvement in reputation and 73% see a significant improvement in relationships. (Figure 4)

ABM delivers significant impact

In which of the following areas have you seen measurable business improvement due to ABM?

73%	65%	40%
Relationships	**Revenue**	**Reputation**
(Account engagement, relationship strength, breadth/ depth of relationships)	*(Revenue per account, pipeline growth, deal size, portfolio penetration)*	*(Brand equity, perception, awareness, and knowledge)*

FIGURE 4

Source: *Momentum ITSMA ABM Benchmarking Study*

3. Technology makes Account-Based Marketing easier

The evolution of marketing and sales technology and tools makes it easier than ever to design, implement, and track account-based efforts. When used correctly, intelligence tools and intent data, account planning templates and tools, and sales enablement technology can facilitate the personalization of content and engagement of accounts. In addition, technology can assist in the tracking of engagement and account behavior, as well as the measurement of results. However, technology should be viewed as an enabler. A successful Account-Based Marketing program requires technology to remain a tool and does not become the primary driver of a program.

> *Vendors need to tailor their approach to stakeholders to account for customers' own business and the stakeholder's role within the purchase process.*
>
> **TAKEAWAY**

However, it is important to note that leaders in Account-Based Marketing strategies leverage more sophisticated technologies, moving beyond customer relationship management (CRM) tools to tools that provide insight into buyer intent. Additionally, many clients we speak with are implementing a customer data platform (CDP), which collates data from multiple tools so you can get a single unified view of all the data on each of your accounts. In addition to using more sophisticated tools, the most successful firms tend to use technology to its full potential. (Figure 5)

The use of tools and tech by ABM leaders

To what extent are you leveraging these tools to their full potential?	ABM Leaders		All Others	
	N	Mean Rating	N	Mean Rating
Events	50	3.9*	66	3.4*
Customer Relationship Management (CRM)	58	3.9*	116	3.5*
Email	60	3.9*	112	3.4*
Marketing Automation System (MAS)	39	3.9*	69	3.4*
Advertising	36	3.8*	76	3.3*
Website	55	3.7*	93	3.4
Engagement Insights	36	3.7*	42	3.0*
Analytics	51	3.6*	71	2.9*
Intent	33	3.6*	60	2.9*
Social	54	3.5	76	3.3
Account Insights	48	3.5*	73	2.9*
Direct Mail	40	3.4*	55	2.8*
ABM Platform	34	3.4*	60	2.8*
Attribution & Reporting	38	3.4*	53	2.6*
Third Party Data	34	3.2	47	3.1

Note: Mean based on a 5-point scale where 1=Just scratching the surface and 5=Fully leveraging the tool's capabilities. Showing the top 15 technologies. *Indicates a statistically significant difference. Source: ITSMA and ABM Leadership Alliance 2021 ABM Benchmark Study, September 2021

FIGURE 5

Source: *Momentum ITSMA ABM Benchmarking Study (ABX), 2021*

The benefits for your customers, teams and company

The value of Account-Based Marketing can be seen in how it breaks down these barriers across a variety of audiences:

Your customers	• Conversations focus more on them than on you • Customers feel better understood as a result of your in-depth analysis and understanding • You provide fresh perspectives and they gain a deeper understanding of your offerings, strategy, and solutions on their terms • Your tailored approach inspires an increase in customer satisfaction and experience • You enable your customers to do the selling and marketing for you, with more customers positioning and selling you across their organization as a partner relevant to their needs
Your teams	• Increase ROI for your customers • Achieve alignment within the account team, with agreement on priorities and value proposition • Create a more unified customer experience with one message and orchestrated experience • Have richer conversations focused on customer needs • Shift perception of your company from vendor to trusted partner and advisor • Uncover new opportunities, extend reach into the customer, and accelerate customer buying cycles • Increase revenue, margin, and wallet share

Your organization	• Align your go-to-market teams around your customers, with no silos
	• Grow your most valuable relationships
	• Improve account penetration, uncover opportunities for cross and upsell
	• Improve market perception
	• Become easier to do business with
	• More consistent in your go-to-market strategy and execution
	• Cut through market noise and differentiate
	• Customers are more inclined to provide references

What do customers on the receiving end think of ABM?

"The magic of Account-Based Marketing is personalization that increases stakeholders engagement across large companies. Having a crisp execution and measurement process for this is essential to success. We have found with financial services that our customers are incredibly receptive especially if we focus on relevance content for them."

– Margaret Franco, Chief Marketing Officer, Finastra

3 The impact of Account-Based Marketing strategies

As organizations embed account-based strategies company-wide, it evolves from a marketing and sales program to a corporate strategy for growth. Building upon core Account-Based Marketing principles of client-centricity, account insights, and collaboration with sales and other entities, it's connected to all the different ways the company is seeking to grow.

Done right, Account-Based Marketing leads to significantly higher ROI than any other marketing approach (Figure 3). And it does more than add to revenues; Account-Based Marketing works to strengthen relationships, grow pipeline, and influence the ways a company goes to market.

If 80 percent of our revenue comes from 20 percent of our customers, then why aren't we focusing efforts on them?

Research shows that Account-Based Marketing is most successful for companies that are looking to:

- Improve account penetration and uncover opportunities for cross-selling and upselling
- Change perceptions or positioning
- Pursue major opportunities
- Develop net new accounts (Figure 6)

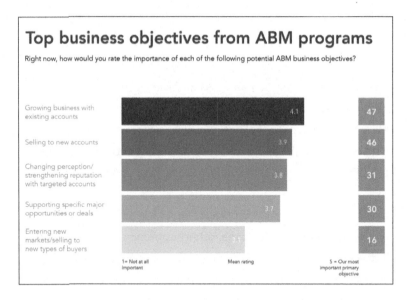

Top business objectives from ABM programs

Right now, how would you rate the importance of each of the following potential ABM business objectives?

	Mean rating	5 = Our most important primary objective
Growing business with existing accounts	4.1	47
Selling to new accounts	3.9	46
Changing perception/strengthening reputation with targeted accounts	3.8	31
Supporting specific major opportunities or deals	3.7	30
Entering new markets/selling to new types of buyers	3.1	16

1 = Not at all Important

FIGURE 6

Source: *Momentum ITSMA ABM Benchmarking Study*

How to measure results

There are three fundamental challenges that all organizations face in delivering and demonstrating the powerful returns that Account-Based Marketing can generate. First, they must accurately measure and evaluate the return on investment (ROI) of Account-Based Marketing programs. Second, they must establish a point of comparison to other growth programs. Finally, and perhaps most importantly, any organization undertaking Account-Based Marketing must set realistic expectations with all stakeholders of the timescales required to achieve results. This is particularly important given that, in many organizations, there is pressure for short-term results. The request to "generate more qualified leads this quarter" is a familiar one. However, Account-Based Marketing is not a short-term lead generation approach. It is a strategic initiative that requires sustained investment to deliver maximum results.

> *Account-Based Marketing is not a short-term lead generation approach. It is a strategic initiative that requires sustained investment to deliver maximum results.*
>
> TAKEAWAY

An Account-Based Marketing program should regularly track performance at both the program level and the account level.

Measurement framework

For years, we have espoused measuring Account-Based Marketing across three priorities that matter most to business: Reputation, Relationships, and Revenue (the 3 Rs):

- **Reputation**, which may include improving perception and/or educating accounts on your offerings or capabilities, through:

  - Customer showing interest in new offerings
  - Reference ability of account
  - Customer satisfaction score
  - Customer loyalty or net promoter score (NPS)

- **Relationships**, which indicate deeper penetration within accounts, such as:

  - Number of new relationships within account or line of business, both executive and non-executive
  - Number of meetings
  - Event attendance
  - Quality of interactions (Figure 7)

- **Revenue**, including pipeline as well as specific identified sales opportunities and other indicators such as:

  - Revenue growth
  - Win rate
  - Account penetration, cross-sell and/or up-sell
  - Sales velocity

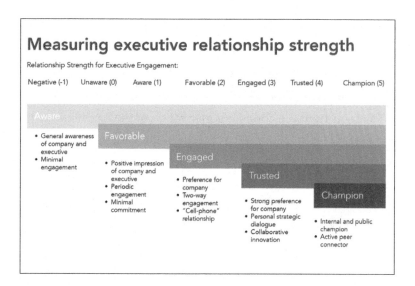

Measuring executive relationship strength

Relationship Strength for Executive Engagement:

Negative (-1)   Unaware (0)   Aware (1)   Favorable (2)   Engaged (3)   Trusted (4)   Champion (5)

Aware
- General awareness of company and executive
- Minimal engagement

Favorable
- Positive impression of company and executive
- Periodic engagement
- Minimal commitment

Engaged
- Preference for company
- Two-way engagement
- "Cell-phone" relationship

Trusted
- Strong preference for company
- Personal strategic dialogue
- Collaborative innovation

Champion
- Internal and public champion
- Active peer connector

FIGURE 7

These metrics are predictors of success, particularly where Account-Based Marketing has not been in place long enough to deliver concrete financial results. What's more, they help to measure how well an Account-Based Marketing initiative is progressing and identify the concrete ways in which Account-Based Marketing is driving business impact.

What results can you expect?

The fifth annual Account-Based Marketing Benchmarking study (ABX) from Momentum ITSMA and the ABM Leadership Alliance, documents both the continued maturation of the discipline and the reality that most programs are still in the early stages of development.

The research was conducted via a qualitative and quantitative study and web-based survey with 300+ Account-Based Marketing leaders and practitioners primarily across technology systems, solutions, and services, software solutions and financial and other business services.

According to 72% of survey respondents, Account-Based Marketing delivers higher ROI than other types of marketing (Figure 3). What's more, 70% say Account-Based Marketing principles influence all of marketing, and nearly half (49%) say Account-Based Marketing plays a major role in making the entire company more customer-centric.

Marketers also report improvement across all three Rs of strategic marketing: relationships, reputation and revenue. (Figure 8)

ABM programs improve the three Rs

% Reporting improvement from ABM

73%

Reputation

(Brand equity, perception, awareness, and knowledge)

65%

Relationships

(Account engagement, relationship strength, breadth/ depth of relationships)

40%

Revenue

(Revenue per account, pipeline growth, deal size, portfolio penetration)

FIGURE 8

Source: *Momentum ITSMA ABM Benchmarking Study*

4 Lessons learned from designing and implementing programs

With the hype about Account-Based Marketing and the strong results it can deliver, it's easy to think it can be all things to all companies. It can't.

To clear up the inevitable confusion and misconceptions about Account-Based Marketing, we are debunking the top three Account-Based Marketing myths we've encountered over the past two decades:

Myth 1: Account-Based Marketing is a personalization tool

Given the explosive growth of Martech vendors positioning their products as account-based tools and marketing agencies positioning personalized campaigns as Account-Based Marketing, it's easy to assume that Account-Based Marketing is synonymous with personalization.

True Account-Based Marketing is not a standalone marketing campaign, even if you happen to use your target's first name in your content. Account-Based Marketing is not about transactions; it's about transformation. It requires collaboration with other groups to customize, personalize, and create relevant experiences so you can truly connect with your target account.

Additionally, accounts do not live in a vacuum. Chances are, individuals at accounts are going to be exposed to a variety of "personalized" outbound and inbound marketing programs coming from other marketing teams across your company, whether they are industry marketing, sales teams, or field marketing. It's essential that an Account-Based Marketing program orchestrates all these touchpoints.

TAKEAWAY

Given the market demand, we're seeing explosive growth of Martech vendors repositioning their tools as Account-Based Marketing tools and marketing agencies positioning their personalized campaign services as Account-Based Marketing. While these tools and tactics can help, buyer beware. They don't bring the knowledge, leadership, and capabilities needed to truly embed Account-Based Marketing principles in an organization.

While technology is essential to personalized marketing and targeted campaigns can be very effective in connecting with customers, it's important to remember that these are enablers, and by themselves, they do not constitute an Account-Based Marketing program. Without the knowledge, insight, and capabilities to truly embed an Account-Based Marketing strategy into an organization, these tools and tactics will fall flat.

Account-Based Marketing is about going to market differently. It is not a marketing or sales tactic or even a set of tactics; it is a *strategy* to build sustained growth with accounts through long-term relationships and value creation. An account-based program is a transformation initiative to drive growth. It shifts the organizational focus from inside-out to outside-in, starting with the account and its problems and opportunities, then working back to how your company can help.

True Account-Based Marketing is not a standalone marketing campaign, even if you happen to use your target's first name in your content.

TAKEAWAY

Myth 2: Account-Based Marketing is a one-size-fits-all solution

Account-Based Marketing truly delivers value time and again for firms with complex propositions, with customers who are complicated either in scale or in the way they make purchasing decisions, or for accounts that are looking for enterprise-wide solutions. It's a strategic, often transformational program that makes sense in long buying cycles with multiple decision-makers.

Account-Based Marketing is a business strategy, not a sales or marketing campaign, and it requires an investment in time, resources, and budget. It is best used with those accounts that can provide a suitable ROI, where you are showing true insight and your service offerings solve a nagging problem or open an avenue to a new opportunity. Thus, Account-Based Marketing is definitely not appropriate for every customer or target account.

If your sales process hinges more on transactions or one-time sales, if you have simple and short sales cycles, or if your buyers are typically very small companies, Account-Based Marketing may be overengineered for you.

TAKEAWAY

Account-Based Marketing is a business strategy, not a sales or marketing campaign and is definitely not appropriate for every customer or target account.

Myth 3: Account-Based Marketing is just another name for Key Account Management

Account-Based Marketing is closely aligned with key or strategic account management (KAM/SAM), but they are not the same thing. At its best, a key account plan operates like a business plan. It includes objectives, sales targets, positioning, delivery, and dependencies. But these account plans often lack specific account value propositions, buyer insights, and marketing plans.

Account-Based Marketing brings together the very best of sales account management with strategic marketing planning. It is this holistic, targeted approach to key accounts that sets Account-Based Marketing apart.

When account teams embed Account-Based Marketing principles and rich account insights, they can move beyond a singular opportunity focus to spot new, potentially lucrative areas of focus that add value to the customer. An Account-Based Marketing program ensures that account teams have the right value propositions and the right content to set the intention for and deliver to the account. By leveraging insight to understand what is most important to decision-makers and influencers, account teams can deliver what their customers need to make the right decisions. Through Account-Based Marketing, marketing fills the gaps in key account management by helping the account team define priorities and identify the "big bets" that can help them achieve their revenue goals.

Multiple Account-Based Marketing programs can exist within a company, as they are designed to support different geographies or business units, and applied at different depths. For strategic accounts, we recommend building one cohesive program for the company, which can lead to better collaboration around accounts, the sharing of assets and learning, and buying efficiencies.

What's the key mindset shift teams need to make when adopting ABM?

"The key is to understand your customers drivers and their considerations, and then try and find a way forward that allows them to feel part of the journey you want to take them on."
    – James Cardew, Chief Marketing Officer, Capital Group

5 Designing your Account-Based Marketing strategy

When designing an Account-Based Marketing strategy that is right for your business, a simple guide is to mirror the way the account coverage model works across tiers of new and existing accounts.

However, Account-Based Marketing is not right for every account. It's a strategy that works best to transform your relationship with a customer; it is not transactional. Given this context, you need to be wary of moving away from the foundational focus on a limited list of key accounts. Many marketing, business, and sales leaders want to apply the Account-Based Marketing approach across hundreds, or even thousands of accounts, but this could dilute your efforts and the results.

Thus, when you're designing an Account-Based Marketing strategy for your business, it is essential to apply Account-Based Marketing principles to your accounts. Those principles are:

- Customer-centricity is paramount
- Insight is needed to build relevance
- Collaboration across the organization is essential
- Account-Based Marketing is not just driving revenue; strengthening reputation and deepening relationships build a focus on customer lifetime value.

With these principles in mind, and in alignment with your company's growth objectives and sales and account management strategy, you need to decide how deep to go with your Account-Based Marketing program.

TAKEAWAY

Account-Based Marketing is not right for every account. It's a strategy that works best to transform your relationship with a customer; it is not transactional.

Strategic account selection

Account-Based Marketing is a strategic growth strategy, so it is most appropriate to build an Account-Based Marketing program for your most strategic accounts that also have the highest potential for growth. The first, and arguably most important step when implementing an Account-Based Marketing program is account selection.

Generally speaking, Account-Based Marketing is best suited for organizations that sell high-cost, high-value, high-consideration solutions. And it makes the most sense to target top-tier accounts that are so important they make or break your future business. Another way of looking at this is to assess the lifetime value of the customer. Your goal should be to either grow or defend your share of wallet at that account. Because Account-Based Marketing is a long-term, resource-intensive bet, it only makes sense to apply it to your most strategic, highest-value accounts.

Highly-customized growth plans for individual accounts

Another critical factor to remember when designing an Account-Based Marketing program is the fact that Account-Based Marketing is done *with* customers, not *to* them. You want to drive value for both companies.

Account teams build stronger relationships with their most valued customers and prospects via highly relevant interactions that demonstrate an in-depth understanding of their business issues. That's why a key principle of Account-Based Marketing is to have a dedicated, senior-level marketer work directly with key account teams on the sales side. Together, they craft fully customized marketing plans and programs for each individual account as an integral part of the overall account plan.

TAKEAWAY

Adopt Account-Based Marketing principles to challenge the conventional ways sales and marketing teams work together to become more relevant to customers and create sustained growth.

Leveraging technology for account insight, developing targeted communications, and tracking progress are only part of the Account-Based Marketing leader's role. The ability to use these insights to create tailored value propositions, relevant thought leadership content and meaningful relationship initiatives set successful Account-Based Marketing leaders apart. And, once the relationship is cemented, teams can focus on creating value by developing new offerings or innovative solutions that customers demand. (Figure 9)

Buyers are seeing innovation & collaboration

% Ranking as "agree" and "strongly agree"

69%	74%	81%
I'm more willing to share information with providers	We have more need to tap providers for innovative thinking	We are more interested in collaborating with providers

FIGURE 9

Source: *Momentum ITSMA CBX, 2022*

Marketing, sales and delivery team collaboration

Account-Based Marketing also demands collaboration between sales and marketing if it is to be successful. Often, this partnership focuses mainly on key decision points, such as

- Which accounts to target,
- Which business problems to solve or opportunities to highlight,
- Which offerings to promote, and
- How to tailor existing content for these programs and campaigns.

Technology can help to automate the account insight process, campaign execution, and measurement of results. Adopting Account-Based Marketing principles can allow you to cover more accounts with the same level of resources, so it is often attractive as companies want to scale beyond the smaller set of strategic accounts. However, the returns for any individual account will, of course, likely be "lite" as well.

Account-Based Marketing for multiple accounts

Companies already engaged in Account-Based Marketing for their strategic accounts often move to embed Account-Based Marketing principles into small groups of accounts that share similar business attributes, challenges, and initiatives, to extend their initial success. Other companies start with this approach to begin with, then transition to a more customized, account-based strategy.

There are times when it makes sense to apply Account-Based Marketing in more than one account at the same time. For example:

- The targeted accounts are large and strategic, but your organization is unable to support the account teams on a one-to-one basis for any reason, such as resource or budget constraints or a lack of sales or senior management buy-in.
- The targeted accounts are characterized as second-tier accounts that, while they don't warrant the same investment you're making in top-tier accounts, are still significant, are high value, help you break into a new market, or offer the opportunity to develop an innovative solution.

In these cases, when you apply Account-Based Marketing principles and success follows, you will likely get management buy-in and the resources you need to fully implement a strategic Account-Based Marketing approach to individual high-value accounts.

When implementing Account-Based Marketing on multiple accounts rather than on an account-by-account basis, it's tempting to keep metrics simple and focused on revenue. Yet, to truly leverage the investment in Account-Based Marketing and keep to the core principles, key metrics for the program should also include brand perception, breadth and depth of relationships, new solution development, business collaboration, and customer advocacy.

What impact has ABM had for you?

"With the advancements in marketing technology, we have so much information at our fingertips it's easy to get lost in the data and lose sight of the customer. Our ABM program helps build deeper customer understanding and connected customer outcomes. It also helps me drive innovation as I look to evolve marketing's role."

**– Sydne Mullings, General Manager, US Central
Marketing Organization, Microsoft**

6 Critical success factors

Account-Based Marketing is a complex business strategy designed to accelerate growth. While the Account-Based Marketing principles are somewhat simple and straightforward, there are seven dimensions that underpin successful programs. Within each dimension, there are three critical success factors that evolve to support the Account-Based Marketing program as it becomes more embedded in the business. (Figure 10)

7 dimensions of successful ABM programs

Strategic & sales alignment	Objectives & metrics	Account selection & segmentation	Program operations & resources	Content & campaigns	Data, analytics & insight	Technology infrastructure
Sponsorships & governance	Strategic objectives	Selection process	Staffing & skills	Messaging & content	Market & account insight	Martech foundation & roadmap
Sales alignment	Metric selection	Selection criteria	Funding & budgeting	Multichannel orchestration	Performance optimization	Account-based engagement
Client-centric orchestration	Tracking & reporting	Account coverage model	Ecosystem management	Customization & personalization	Strategic planning	Campaign activation

FIGURE 10

Source: © 2022. Momentum ITSMA ABM Adoption Model. All rights reserved.

Dimension 1: Strategic Alignment

It's important to have the right overall sponsorship and governance of your Account-Based Marketing program and to position it as a business imperative rather than a marketing program. When a program is embraced by executives, it is far easier to drive collaboration throughout the rest of the organization. Particularly for Account-Based Marketing, alignment is critical, not just in the process and tools used, but also in a client-centric mindset and culture across the business. This is a fundamental aspect of Account-Based Marketing, as a lack of alignment leads to a subsequent lack of buy-in from teams, and ultimately, to a struggling program.

The three critical success factors for this dimension are:

4. **Sponsorship and governance.** Successful embedded Account-Based Marketing programs are sponsored and supported by executive management. While Account-Based Marketing programs are typically driven, sponsored, and governed by marketing, once it is embedded as a strategic change program, the strategy should sit closely within the wider business planning process.

5. **Sales, marketing & delivery team alignment.** While alignment between teams begins with tactical, joint activities, as Account-Based Marketing expands, teams should have shared expectations, targets, and responsibilities. Program leaders should provide support for integrated planning and

orchestration, and sponsor joint training in Account-Based Marketing and sales methodologies to foster alignment.

6. **Client-centric orchestration.** At the exploring stage, the mindset of the business is often "inside-out" — what we want to sell the customer— rather than client-centric. When Account-Based Marketing is embedded, sales and account management, industry/field marketing, and other customer-facing functions orchestrate their activities for the benefit of the client.

Dimension 2: Objectives and Metrics

Account-Based Marketing program objectives should not just be aligned with company objectives; the company's objectives should drive your Account-Based Marketing program. Through a number of previously agreed-upon metrics, organizations can track improvements in reputation, relationships, and revenue growth within the prioritized accounts. Critical success factors are:

1. **Strategic objectives.** You should have different objectives depending on which phase of Account-Based Marketing adoption you're in. If you're exploring, you need to prove that Account-Based Marketing is a viable strategy. When experimenting and expanding, your objectives will be tied to specific accounts or campaigns. Once the program is embedded, the program objectives are synonymous with your strategic business goals. Thus, Account-Based Marketing will eventually influence the way wider sales and marketing objectives are set and how metrics are tracked and reported.

2. **Metric selection.** During pilots, metrics are often activity-focused rather than outcome-based. Sales usage of marketing assets is tracked, and anecdotal account team or customer feedback is collected. As the program scales across the business, output and outcome-based metrics across the three categories of reputation, relationships, and revenue are tracked and measured.

3. **Approaches to tracking and reporting.** When you're exploring Account-Based Marketing, you define results that will prove the concept. Ultimately, performance is tracked and reported at a program level, by type of Account-Based Marketing in use, and on an account, cluster, or group basis.

Dimension 3: Account selection and segmentation

It's easy to see how these dimensions build off one another. Account selection and segmentation require significant collaboration between sales and marketing as well as the wider business, which is why it's important to first create cross-functional alignment and then establish agreed-upon metrics. To select, prioritize, and segment accounts, all teams need to be rowing in the same direction. Success factors for account selection include:

1. **The selection process itself.** During a pilot, it's easiest to begin with the account team's existing list of key, strategic, and/or targeted accounts. As Account-Based Marketing expands, marketing can leverage its evidence-based insights to have more influence over the way accounts are selected. Together, marketing and sales teams can implement a formal account selection process involving propensity modeling and strategic fit data.

2. **Criteria for selection.** Again, this process will evolve as an Account-Based Marketing program matures. Initially, existing accounts with potential for increased growth or high potential target accounts will be the top priority. As the program expands, accounts are assigned Account-Based Marketing resources if they meet agreed account selection criteria and internal conditions.

3. **Account coverage model**. Existing sales coverage models are used to guide early plans for Account-Based Marketing. To expand the program, sales and marketing work together to organize accounts into defined tiers within a joint coverage model. Ultimately, the account prioritization model is collaboratively developed and is supported by technology.

Dimension 4: Content and campaigns

Campaign planning and execution, message development, and content creation are the foundations of marketing. However, the challenge to develop account and stakeholder insights, to customize assets to increase relevancy, to orchestrate multichannel campaigns that drive seamless online and offline engagement, and to coordinate efforts across multiple teams, makes Account-Based Marketing a far more sophisticated and complex strategic program.

The success of content and campaigns depends on:

1. **Leveraging existing messaging and content.** Especially during the pilot phase, teams brainstorm a list of potential campaign tactics and assets for each account. As the program expands, content assets are created specifically for accounts, clusters, or groups, and are pushed back into a central toolkit for further reuse and customization by the wider marketing team.

2. **Multichannel orchestration.** The strength of an Account-Based Marketing program is orchestration. On one level, it needs to coordinate sales, marketing, and other elements of campaign execution in a seamless, integrated experience. To truly add value, Account-Based Marketing teams must also orchestrate the wider business's interactions with accounts and influence other initiatives such as advocacy or customer success programs.

3. **Customization and personalization.** The customization and personalization of content evolve as an Account-Based Marketing program matures. During exploration, personalized tactics are planned for each Account-Based Marketing approach. For pilots, existing content is personalized to target stakeholders and buyer personas. When the program expands, a project management office (PMO) or center of excellence (CoE) provides Account-Based Marketing teams with a centralized resource. Localization and personalization of content are managed by each individual.

Dimension 5: Program operations and resources

Once the business sees the impact that Account-Based Marketing can have on accounts, demand for Account-Based Marketing support grows at a rate that outstrips what the existing Account-Based Marketing team can supply. Thus, one of the most enduring challenges facing Account-Based Marketing program leaders is how to resource and fund a program to meet the needs of the business.

It takes focus on three key areas to do this successfully:

1. **Staffing and skills**. Pilots are staffed with existing marketers with the most appropriate skills, such as field marketing. To expand the program, a central PMO/CoE supports Account-Based Marketing leads aligned to market units. Mature, successful Account-Based Marketing programs identify competencies, create job roles and families, and offer formal professional development and mentoring to support career development. The goal is to create a consistent approach and provide continuing professional development to deliver on the program.

2. **Funding and budgets**. Initial funding is secured as a special project or from existing marketing budgets. Funding for scaling may come from a combination of marketing, sales, and business unit budgets, with PMO/CoE oversight or control. Once embedded, Account-Based Marketing is a strategic investment by the business and budgets are protected, controlled, or monitored by the central PMO/CoE team.

3. **Ecosystem management**. Individuals leading the pilot planning process work on their own with little collaboration from other marketing groups or the wider business. As the program expands, an ecosystem of agencies, technology providers, and consultants is selected to support a standardized approach, achieving economies of scale for the business.

Dimension 6: Data, Analytics, and Insight

Account-Based Marketing is built on customer insight—it's one of the four guiding principles for this strategic approach. The use of data to build market and account insights, optimize performance, and inform strategic planning for the Account-Based Marketing program and wider business initiatives can be a competitive advantage, and is evolving as marketing functions in general become more data-driven.

Account-Based Marketing programs are increasingly expected to be data-savvy in three specific areas:

1. **Market and account insights.** When exploring Account-Based Marketing, marketing takes an inventory of existing sources of account insight and identifies gaps to be addressed before pilots can begin. Once Account-Based Marketing is embedded, advanced insight tools are consistently used, integrating data from multiple sources and using automated analytics to deliver timely insights.

2. **Performance optimization.** When piloting, teams work with internal data analytics resources to extract what is needed from internal systems while using third-party subscriptions and databases to supplement where required. As the program expands, third-party data is integrated with internal data to provide a more complete view of target account engagement and intent. Performance dashboards are standard practice and support an agile approach to Account-Based Marketing.

3. **Strategic planning.** In the early stages of an Account-Based Marketing program, it's common to rely on historic data and sales knowledge to make strategic decisions about the design of the Account-Based Marketing program. However, as Account-Based Marketing becomes embedded, sales uses Account-Based Marketing insights to adjust plans and activities for their key accounts and other executives use the insights generated by the Account-Based Marketing program to make strategic business decisions.

Dimension 7: Technology Infrastructure

The lines between marketing and technology are blurred. Account-Based Marketing is considered a category of marketing technology, and all business leaders constantly try to keep pace with the latest technologies to support their programs, while understanding how they might fit with the company's existing IT infrastructure. When adopting Account-Based Marketing technology, it's important to remember that technology is an enabler that improves efficiencies, increases impact, and aligns teams. It is not, in and of itself, a solution.

There are three ways to use technology to best support the Account-Based Marketing program:

1. **Foundations and roadmap.** Specific Account-Based Marketing tools can be implemented during pilots as long as they fit in the wider marketing technology roadmap. Once Account-Based Marketing is embedded and becomes part of the company's overall strategy, Account-Based Marketing technologies should become a core part of the corporate Martech stack and technology providers should be seen as integral to the wider ecosystem supporting the global Account-Based Marketing team.

2. **Account-based engagement.** Technology gaps between marketing and sales often prevent collaboration at scale. To expand Account-Based Marketing, dedicated teams access a rich pool of information via platforms that offer account insight in real time, until finally, technology is used by all

functions for improved insight, targeting, planning, and personalization for Account-Based Marketing accounts pre- and post-sale.

3. **Campaign activation.** When scaling Account-Based Marketing, technology is used to serve up personalized content in sophisticated nurture flows. Ultimately, technology is widely used across the Account-Based Marketing program: stakeholder profiling, intent tracking, social media targeting and content personalization, and digital "always on" activity are being managed centrally.

7 How to embed an Account-Based Marketing strategy

The best Account-Based Marketing programs start by making sure that all internal stakeholders really know what the approach is, why the organization is investing in it, and how to implement and run a successful Account-Based Marketing program. It is essential to take the time upfront to clear confusion and hype and make sure that everyone involved in this important business growth initiative understands and agrees on how the Account-Based Marketing process can drive customer success and deliver other business objectives for existing and new accounts.

Beyond the Account-Based Marketing fundamentals, your stakeholders need to think hard about how best to apply Account-Based Marketing principles to their specific business model, market context, and sales strategy. This will depend on your offering, account base, and the culture/skillset of your teams.

Once your organization has decided how to apply Account-Based Marketing, it is imperative that the program gets the investment, resources, and continuous focus required to align the initiative with the account's buying process. While we have been Account-Based Marketing-centric for decades, the reality is that Account-Based Marketing is still a fairly new or misunderstood initiative for most companies. Once the initial excitement passes, the hard work of ongoing collaboration across the company begins. To ensure you reap the full benefits of Account-Based Marketing, you must remain focused on the implementation of integrated programs and campaigns across marketing and sales, while increasing your connection with delivery and customer success teams and programs to accelerate growth and maximize the lifetime value of each target account.

Despite the ongoing hard work, Account-Based Marketing is worth the cultural adjustment and the investment. Here's what Account-Based Marketing can do:

1. **Deliver higher returns:** Identifying high-value accounts, understanding their needs and opportunities, offering personalized solutions, and investing time to nurture customers in an orchestrated way across your organization offers the potential to reap far greater rewards than you would with conventional siloed marketing and sales programs.

2. **Strengthen and sustain relationships:** When you truly understand your customer's needs and those of their customer, it demonstrates your commitment to their success,

strengthens your relationship, and lays the groundwork for a long-term, sustainable, mutually beneficial partnership.

3. **Help close complex deals:** Many high-worth deals involve multiple decision-makers from across the customer organization, each with their own perspective. This requires a deep, data-driven understanding of the customer, patience for a long sales cycle, and a willingness to show the customer that their needs are your top priority. When you apply Account-Based Marketing principles to key accounts, you build the credibility and trust you need to close complicated deals.

4. **Provide the opportunity to up-sell and cross-sell:** Account-Based Marketing arms you with evidence-based insights and helps you earn trust with the customer so it is easier to identify other opportunities in the account where partnering makes sense for both of you.

5. **Fuel innovation; yours and your customer's:** When you truly understand the customer's priorities, issues, opportunities, organization, and inner workings, and you've developed a deep trust, you have the opportunity to work together to develop future products and services that help your customer strategically grow their business.

Beyond the Account-Based Marketing fundamentals, your stakeholders need to think hard about how best to apply Account-Based Marketing principles to their specific business model, market context, and sales strategy.

TAKEAWAY

Each of these benefits corresponds to a different phase in the Account-Based Marketing adoption journey (Figure 11):

- Exploring
- Experimenting
- Expanding
- Embedded

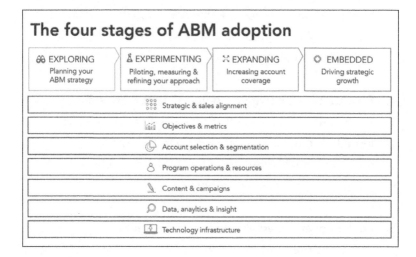

FIGURE 11

Source: © 2022. Momentum ITSMA ABM Adoption Model. All rights reserved.

Stage 1. Exploring

During the exploring stage, the focus is on first answering the question, "Could Account-Based Marketing work for us?" If the answer is yes, you then need to determine the right Account-Based Marketing approach to support your business's growth agenda and go-to-market strategy.

Typically, individual marketers or business unit leaders who are leading the Account-Based Marketing charge drive this planning, gaining buy-in from key stakeholders and conducting initial research to identify the best approach. This determination is based upon the business's average deal size, length of the sales cycle, potential annual customer revenues, and sales coverage model. At this stage, you may be required to build a business case internally for investment.

Once this initial research is complete and the business case is approved, it's time to move to stage two, experimenting, where you move Account-Based Marketing from theory into practice.

Stage 2. Experimenting

During the experimenting stage, Account-Based Marketing leaders pilot, measure, and refine the approach. Prior to starting, it's helpful to gain the commitment of both sales and business unit leadership so they actively support the necessary collaboration between marketing, sales, customer success, and other teams that touch the selected accounts, clusters, or target groups.

The experimenting process itself is straightforward: conduct the pilots, track the results, and refine the activities as needed. If the pilot is successful, the next step is to make a business case for scaling Account-Based Marketing.

Often, organizations find that Account-Based Marketing shows such a positive impact on the business in terms of stronger relationships, better reputation, and growing opportunities and revenues, that they face a new challenge: keeping up with demand for Account-Based Marketing support from other sales teams and account managers, and other areas of the business.

This drives the move to stage three, expansion of the program.

> **TAKEAWAY**
>
> *Often, organizations find that Account-Based Marketing shows such a positive impact on the business in terms of stronger relationships, better reputation, and growing opportunities and revenues, that they face a new challenge: keeping up with demand for Account-Based Marketing support.*

Stage 3. Expanding

Expanding your Account-Based Marketing program means you're increasing the program account coverage either within an industry or across a business line. This is when it's essential to follow a standardized approach, so you can operate at scale, with greater efficiencies and better integration and collaboration across the business.

When program expansion leads to an improved business line in one area of the business, leaders from other areas of the organization are sure to catch wind of it. Account-Based Marketing will undoubtedly capture the attention of the executives in the wider organization and they will want to be part of it.

This is an opportunity to position Account-Based Marketing as a strategic growth driver for the business and embed it across the organization.

And while this may seem like an easy win, it's a good idea to treat this almost as another pilot. To fully embed an Account-Based Marketing program requires each team to embrace the principles of Account-Based Marketing and potentially change the way they have always managed their accounts. This type of change may not work for each team; it may be too expensive, or it may not add enough value to fully embed Account-Based Marketing across the organization, at least, not immediately.

Stage 4. Embedded

If, however, your company is ready to embrace Account-Based Marketing as the primary strategy to drive growth across your business, it's time to get busy.

Account-Based Marketing can revolutionize the way your company goes to market and delivers customer success. It requires a continual focus on account prioritization, research, investment, customer engagement, and sales collaboration. When Account-Based Marketing is embedded, you are looking to drive innovation with your target accounts.

8 How to accelerate your Account-Based Marketing

At first glance, the Account-Based Marketing adoption model can appear overwhelming (Figure 11). However, taking a rigorous approach to assessing where your program falls in each of the three main factors within each of the seven dimensions can accelerate your Account-Based Marketing success.

That's why we have developed the Account-Based Marketing Accelerator (Figure 12), a rapid diagnostic process to help assess capabilities across your company compared to a benchmark of comparable organizations. When we apply the Account-Based Marketing accelerator, we also identify recommendations for advancing your program and increasing your impact.

Using an Account-Based Marketing assessment, we measure organizations against the four stages of program adoption, together with seven dimensions and the 21 success factors that are critical to advancing an Account-Based Marketing strategy across the business.

This tool explores the main factors within each of the seven dimensions to give businesses a detailed gap analysis and recommendations for advancing their programs and increasing their impact.

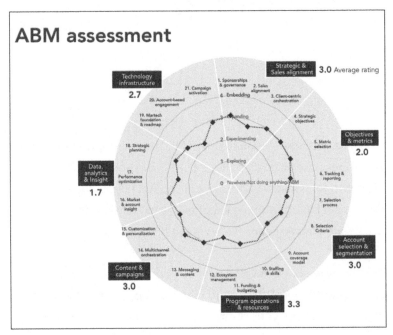

··◆·· Best-in-class Companies (N=9)

FIGURE 12 Momentum ITSMA Account-Based Growth Accelerator

Source: © 2022. Momentum ITSMA ABM Assessment. All rights reserved.

Maturity matters

It's important to build your strategy for the long haul if you're to see the full impact of the program. Results typically improve as programs mature, with programs at the expanding and embedding stages scoring considerably higher in account team satisfaction, engagement in accounts, pipeline, and revenue growth (Figure 13).

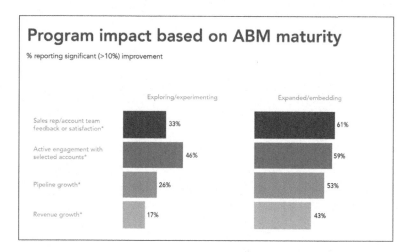

FIGURE 13

Source: *Momentum ITSMA ABM Benchmarking Study (ABX), 2021*

Account-Based Marketing leaders see significantly more success and business improvements than other firms. Typically, these leaders see 84% growth in revenue vs. 53% (Figure 14).

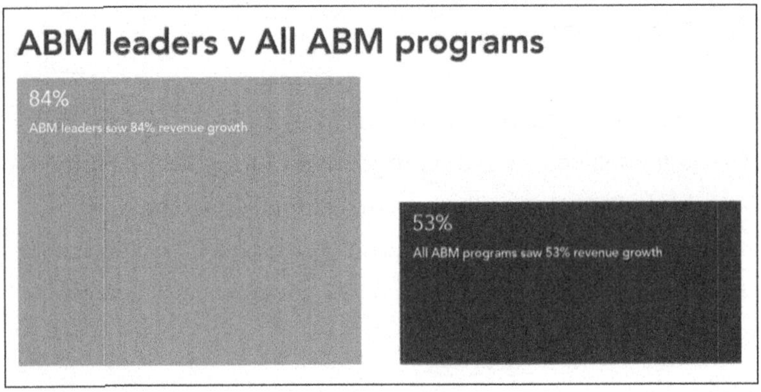

ABM leaders v All ABM programs

84%
ABM leaders saw 84% revenue growth

53%
All ABM programs saw 53% revenue growth

FIGURE 14

Source: *Momentum ITSMA ABM Benchmarking Study (ABX), 2021*

Why do ABM programs need to keep evolving?

"Companies that make bolder moves during times of huge change are the ones that out-perform their peers. Be bold, open up a new channel, experiment with options, figure out how to deliver a truly omnichannel, integrated experience for your accounts and don't expect that the status quo will be what's needed for success going forward."

– Liz Harrison, Partner, McKinsey

A roadmap for success

Building on our research and experience with customers, we've created this roadmap to help executives implement an account-based program that accelerates business success.

1. Strategic alignment

- Position this as a strategic corporate growth program, not just as an activity or tactic
- Enlist greater involvement in governance from a more diverse group of senior leaders
- Measure and report results, both quantitative and qualitative, using the Three Rs: Reputation, Relationships, and Revenue

2. Sales collaboration

- Collaborate with sales, marketing and delivery teams to fully integrate with the account planning and engagement processes
- Work more closely with the customer at every stage of relationship development
- Educate teams at every step of the way to increase their confidence and build trust

3. Staff development

- Invest in team and individual skill development across a wide range of Account-Based Marketing competencies
- Create formal career paths to support team retention and development
- Use a competency model designed specifically for Account-Based Marketing to prioritize skills, identify skills gaps and plan for professional development to close the gaps

4. Process excellence

- Centralize your program management to achieve scale and embed Account-Based Marketing in your organization
- Invest in tools, templates, and process development to standardize and facilitate reuse
- Build a community approach to share best practices across divisions and business units

5. Technology and data leverage

- Reinforce the tech stack with analytics and insight tools
- Emphasize integration, usability, and adoption to ensure maximum leverage of existing tools and systems
- Invest more in training to ensure confidence and capability with priority data, insight, and tools

About the author

Alisha Lyndon is Chief Executive at Momentum ITSMA. She has 20 years of experience advising technology, professional services, and financial services firms on revenue growth strategies, key account development, and talent.

Having worked for leading technology vendors, including Microsoft and as Managing Director at Logicall, Alisha pioneered the use of Account-Based Marketing (ABM) to drive growth in strategic accounts, founding Momentum – now Momentum ITSMA – and growing it into a world leader in ABM.

Alisha has advised many global enterprises on their ABM programs, including Amazon, Deloitte, Google, Microsoft, and State Street. She is a high-profile speaker on growth topics, hosts the Account-Based Marketing and Breaking the Bias podcasts, and is a regular contributor to Forbes.

About Momentum ITSMA

Momentum ITSMA is a world-leading B2B growth consultancy and analyst firm.

The firm was created in 2021, when ABM-leaders Momentum combined with ITSMA – the leading authority on marketing standards, learning, and effectiveness. Today, we deliver consulting, research, and learning services that help global organizations accelerate revenue through Account-Based Marketing. Our 100+ global team transforms deep market knowledge and IP into hands-on services through four service lines: Growth Consultancy, Growth Intelligence, Growth Academy, and Growth Hub.

With deep experience in tech, financial services, and professional services, we enable clients to embed a customer-first mindset, truly understand their markets, and build the right capabilities. We also empower client teams to drive productivity and effectiveness through the world's most dynamic community of B2B marketers.

Made in the USA
Monee, IL
06 March 2023

29067391R00056